The Desperation Day Book Two

Mary Bramer

SCHOLASTIC BOOK SERVICES

New York Toronto London Auckland Sydney Tokyo

*To all those who helped and
encouraged me in my teaching
but especially to my parents.*

ISBN 0-590-31541-2

12 11 10 9 8 7 6 5 4 3 2 1   10   0 1 2 3 4 5/8

Printed in the U.S.A.   02

TABLE OF CONTENTS

Introduction

WORD WIZARDRY *1*
A Dog Is A Dog Or Is It? 2
Antonym Chains 5
   Sample: Nine Antonym Chains 6
Visual Dictionaries 10
   Sample: Visual Dictionary Sheet 12
Word Beads 14
   Model Spirit Master 1:
   Word Bead Sheet 15
An Affixing Race 17
What Is My Abode? 20
   Model Spirit Master 2:
   Thesaurus Word Search 22
Alive And Well And Hiding In English 23
   Model Spirit Master 3:
   Word Tree Pattern 26
Illustrating Idioms 27

COMPOSITION COLLECTION *30*
Models For Success 31
   Model Spirit Master 4:
   "An Animal I Loved" 33
   Model Spirit Master 5:
   "The Ideal Vacation" 35
A Circle Of Life 36

Mastering Modification 39
    Model Spirit Master 6:
    Three Paragraphs 40
    Model Spirit Master 7:
    Blank Paragraph 42
Unfinished Stories 43
    Model Spirit Master 8:
    Three Stories To Finish 44
Dear Me 48
Writing By Numbers 51
    Model Spirit Master 9:
    Short Story Ingredients Sheet 53
Figuratively Speaking 57
    Model Spirit Master 10:
    Figurative Language Situations 60

MISCELLANEOUS MIX   63
Words In Pictures............................ 64
    Model Spirit Master 11:
    Pictured Words Sheet 65
Rhyme Words 68
Book Report Collages 71
Classifying 74
    Model Spirit Master 12:
    Classification Categories Sheet 76
Do You See What I See? 79
Now Hear This! 82
Experiment In Communication 84

Introduction

For years I have shared teaching ideas with fellow teachers. Several years ago I collected some short lesson plans into a little book called *The Desperation Day Book*. These were all short activities — time-fillers for the end of a class period, expanders to broaden a unit, or whole lessons for one particular day when everything goes wrong. The response to that book was so heartening that I have collected a second group of teaching ideas. These, however, are not necessarily limited to single-day activities. Although many of them can be completed in one class session or less, others slip over into homework assignments or are best used with a follow-up on a second day.

Like the earlier book, this is a collection of lessons you will want to incorporate into your own teaching style. Some ideas are definitely class activities. Others might best be used in lap packs to tempt the individual. For example, a student of lesser abilities might be given a lap-pack folder containing a model composition to copy, a word-beads sheet to practice recognizing words, and the rhyme-words exercise to sharpen spelling. A lap pack to challenge the bright student with time on her hands might contain the classifying exercise, the Latin root word-family tree, and the figurative language sheet. With clean paper tucked inside each lap-pack folder, the student could be off to a study room or the library to work on her own. Some chapters may be used just for the sample hand-out sheets, which can be easily duplicated. Sometimes the chapter activity may be offered as an extra credit opportunity. By typing some of the individual writing activities (figurative language, unfinished stories, etc.) on separate 5″ x 8″ index cards, a good set of composition topics can be prepared for a writing center. Best of all, an idea from this book might be the catalyst that triggers your own creative efforts in a different direction.

Many of these ideas aren't new. In fact, some of them date back to my first year of teaching—twenty years ago. Others originated only last year. All have been used in my own classroom. They will, however, seem new and original to you only if you have not thought about them before. I hope I have something different to offer. In my earlier book, I suggested that these were the kinds of activities teachers shared over a cup of coffee. Once again I invite you to pour yourself a cup of coffee, and let me share some ideas for teaching language arts.

Mary Bramer

WORD WIZARDRY

I personally dislike teaching vocabulary lessons that consist of lists of words that students look up and learn temporarily to pass a test a few days later. Yet I believe vocabulary building should be incorporated into my teaching. I want my students to enjoy words, to work with them, to see them in new forms and combinations. I have never considered crossword puzzles and other word games as mere time-fillers. I have always encouraged reading as an excellent way to expand vocabulary. The following lessons are based on the premise that what students enjoy, they will do. I hope these simple lessons will offer learning experiences in the guise of word play that will help students find a curiosity for their language and a magic in its use. My ultimate goal is to instill in as many students as possible a lifetime love affair with words.

A Dog Is A Dog Or Is It?

Objective: to understand denotation of words
to understand connotation and shades of meaning
to introduce euphemisms

Materials: nothing special

Procedure: Write the word *dog* on the board and ask for a volunteer to define it as a dictionary might. Others may revise, limit, or add to the definition. You might have someone check an actual dictionary entry to see how accurate the class's definition is. Then explain that the class has just demonstrated the denotation of the word — its exact, literal meaning. All words have a denotative meaning.

However, through use and time some words take on a positive or negative shade of meaning called *connotation.* Although *dog* is a fairly uncolored term, to the animal lover it has a positive meaning. A person frightened of dogs will associate negative synonyms. Few, if any, synonyms have identical meanings. Through the choice of synonyms, color or shading can be given to speech and writing. For example, a career government employee can be called a *politician* or a *statesman.* Basically, the two words mean the same thing. But their connotation, or implied meaning, differs. *Politician* seems to mean a more devious or crafty person while *statesman* connotes a more noble leader.

Less similar synonyms or slang words differ even more. For example, *horse,* like *dog,* has very little shading to it. To call the animal a *hayburner,* however, gives a negative interpretation. On the other hand, to call a horse a *thoroughbred* implies it has fine bloodlines.

To further explain this, ask students to contribute at least 24 synonyms for *dog*. If the class is stumped, choose synonyms from the list below:

guide	mutt	friend	pooch
purebred	renegade	mongrel	comrade
cur	barker	hunter	killer
brute	biter	retriever	guardian
fleabag	companion	hound	canine
protector	stray	leader	runt

Each student then divides a piece of scratch paper into two columns — positive and negative. They may list any number of words on either side. When they finish, copy the class's synonyms on the board. Nearly everyone will see that a word like *cur* has a negative connotation, but there may be some disagreement about a word like *hunter*. Some will find it a positive term while others may consider hunting a negative skill. This is a good time to mention that personal values contribute to connotations. Although a word like *crook* has an almost universally negative connotation, this is not true of all words.

In another activity, students draw a continuous line from one side of their paper to the other. They label one end *positive* and the other, *negative*. In the middle of the line they write the word *dog*. Along the line, each student then writes in the other synonyms according to his degree of feeling about the word. The most neutral terms appear near the center of the line and the most positive or negative words, at either end.

negative   dog   positive

Another possibility is to have students place the 24 dog synonyms on a line from worst to best. The whole class ranks them by number from 1 to 25 on the blackboard. At *13,* the exact middle, write the word *dog*. Then ask for suggestions for the worst term and write it in at 25.

While there is no correct order for this, attempting to rank words according to connotations does demonstrate the difficulty of trying to define words precisely.

Variation: When a positive synonym for a word is deliberately used, it is called a *euphemism*. This lesson provides a good opportunity to teach euphemisms. For the sake of courtesy, usually a euphemism replaces an unpleasant term. Some seemingly menial occupations are often given fancy titles to make them sound more important. Terms associated with death are frequently euphemistic.

Students may want to collect euphemisms as a language project. One interesting source is a student's report card. For example, if a teacher writes that a pupil "interacts physically with the classmates near him," the teacher is actually saying he hits students around him. "She's somewhat shy," might mean she hides under the table. A collection of similar comments and their interpretations makes an interesting project.

A study of denotation, connotation, and euphemisms is also a good introduction to a unit on the language of advertising. It also works well as just an interesting aspect of word study.

Antonym Chains

Objective: to reinforce understanding of antonyms

Materials: roll of adding machine paper to type on (optional) hollow tubes [as cut from a roll of kitchen wrap] for storage

Procedure: Word chains may not be the correct name for these little word games, but they seem to be constructed word by word just as a chain is link by link. Although word chains can be put on cards or sheets of paper, it's more interesting to put them on long pieces of adding machine paper and roll them up. The chains can be put on one continuous paper, or they can be divided into two or three separate chains. If no adding machine paper is available, the chains can be typed on ordinary paper, cut into strips, and taped together. The rolls can then be stored in a section of hollow tubing cut from a roll of household wrap or foil. These make excellent additions to a collection of classroom vocabulary builders or learning games. If the antonym chains are divided into more than one long chain, the directions should appear at the beginning of each roll of paper.

Somewhere in your word study you will probably want to talk about synonyms and antonyms. Remind students that antonyms are opposites. To emphasize this, you might say some common words and have students call out antonyms for them. After a few big/little, dark/light, wrinkled/smooth sets, students will have the idea.

You might also want to explain the idea of word chains. The two main things to understand are that only one letter is replaced in each step, and that all the other letters remain in their same positions. Since letters can not be added or removed, antonym chains work only when the antonyms have the same number of letters. Thus a combination like big/little could never be handled in a word chain.

To demonstrate the idea of word chains, the following sample can be done on the chalkboard with the answers written as the clues are read aloud to the class:

1. difficult	hard
2. small piece of pasteboard as for a game	card
3. small, wheeled conveyance	cart
4. a plaster around a broken bone	cast
5. compass direction	east
6. opposite of #1	easy

The reason for doing a class example is to show the two significant characteristics — letter positions are constant and only one letter changes at each step. Once shown to students, some of them may try to build their own antonym chains. This is excellent, as it calls for dictionary work on their part.

The following pages contain a collection of antonym games. At first, the number of letters in the answer is indicated as a help. Obviously, no set number of steps is maintained, just whatever is necessary.

Find the word that matches the first definition and write it on your paper. The next word to match the next definition will use all the same letters in order, *except one* will be replaced. The last word in the series will be the opposite of the first word (antonym). You may use a dictionary.

A *(4 letters)*
1. not well
2. a natural fabric
3. part of a window
4. legal document disposing of property after death
5. opposite of #1

B (4 letters)

1. like strongly
2. be alive
3. bee house
4. possess
5. opposite of #1

C (3 letters)

1. not new
2. Spanish cheer
3. beverage
4. everything, total
5. be sick
6. nothing
7. baby insect
8. negative word
9. currently
10. opposite of #1

D

1. not fast
2. cabbage salad
3. bird's foot
4. applaud
5. loose piece
6. toss around
7. dart quickly
8. level, even
9. daring deed
10. festival like
11. opposite of #1

E

1. dark color
2. cube
3. timepiece
4. stoneware jug
5. wheel wedge
6. baby chicken
7. not thin
8. use thought
9. thy own
10. high-pitched cry
11. opposite of #1

F

1. very big
2. squeezes
3. work boats
4. price labels
5. light browns
6. metal containers
7. opposite of #1

7

G

1. move upward
2. make angry
3. steel tool for smoothing rough edges
4. load up
5. opposite of #1

H

1. a large amount
2. hair on horse's neck
3. narrow path
4. a single, just one
5. opposite of #1

I

1. tiny, little
2. future form for *should*
3. person planted in crowd to start buying at sales, auctions, etc.
4. make colder
5. dialect form of *child*, as in "honey _____"
6. a bell sound heard on some clocks
7. an act against the law
8. French for *cream*
9. small French pancake, usually with a filling
10. past tense of *creep*
11. archaic tense for *crop*
12. a native of Croatia
13. old English silver coin
14. opposite of #1

Variation: You may want to suggest that students try constructing their own word chains. The following pairs are possibilities:

soft/hard	moon/star
rich/poor	sky/sea
music/drama	good/evil

Answers to word chains:

A
1. sick
2. silk
3. sill
4. will
5. well

B
1. love
2. live
3. hive
4. have
5. hate

C
1. old
2. olé
3. ale
4. all
5. ail
6. nil
7. nit
8. not
9. now
10. new

D
1. slow
2. slaw
3. claw
4. clap
5. flap
6. flip
7. flit
8. flat
9. feat
10. fest
11. fast

E
1. black
2. block
3. clock
4. crock
5. chock
6. chick
7. thick
8. think
9. thine
10. whine
11. white

F
1. huge
2. hugs
3. tugs
4. tags
5. tans
6. tins
7. tiny

G
1. rise
2. rile
3. file
4. fill
5. fall

H
1. many
2. mane
3. lane
4. lone
5. none

I
1. small
2. shall
3. shill
4. chill
5. chile
6. chime
7. crime
8. crême
9. crepe
10. crept
11. cropt
12. Croat
13. groat
14. great

Visual Dictionaries

Objective: to illustrate the multiple meanings of certain English words

Materials: several kinds of dictionaries
catalogs, old magazines, and newspapers to cut up
sheets for mounting the visual dictionaries

Procedure: Older students have been using dictionaries for years without consciously being aware of them. Sometimes an upper grade teacher will review the parts of a dictionary to be sure that everyone in the class has been exposed to all the elements that might be encountered in the year's activities. Such a review would probably include the following:

guide words (their purpose)
pronunciation in parentheses (key at bottom)
definitions (numbering, grouping)
parts of speech (abbreviations used)
synonyms (sometimes antonyms)
etymology in brackets (end of entry)
spelling (preferred, irregular forms of plurals)
syllables (for dividing words)

Although such information is important, dictionaries are most often used to find meanings of unfamiliar words. The task is complicated by the fact that some English words have multiple meanings. This activity calls attention to a number of common English words with multiple meanings.

Making a visual dictionary entry is a good activity to follow up a dictionary review. To do this, each student selects a common word with multiple meanings. The following words make good visual entries:

arm	figure	jack	play
base	fine	pad	ring
belt	fire	pan	run
cap	foot	pass	spring
class	free	pen	star
cut	frog	pin	table
drive	hand	plane	trunk
fall	heart	plate	turn

After each student has chosen an entry word (no more than two in a class should have the same word), he collects as many definitions as possible, using more than one dictionary. He may include any definitions marked *colloq.* or *slang.* He should be required to have a minimum of six definitions. Each definition is numbered as the student copies it on scratch paper.

After he has found his definitions, the student locates pictures or makes drawings that illustrate as many definitions as possible. For example, if his word is *belt,* he might cut a picture of a waistband of slacks with the belt clearly visible. From the automotive section of a catalog, he might get a picture of a fan belt. A headline might offer wording similar to the following: "City Demands Developer Provide Green Belt." Since space is limited, small pictures and drawings work best. Nouns are easiest to picture, but some verbs are active enough to illustrate. A student should have a minimum of four pictures. Each picture should be numbered to correspond with a matching definition.

Although words and pictures for a visual dictionary entry can be put together on notebook paper, you might want to duplicate a special sheet like the one on the following page for students to use.

Visual Dictionary

(entry word)

_____
_____
_____
_____
_____
_____
_____
_____
_____
_____

On the blank, each student writes his entry word. Within the frame, pictures and illustrations can be pasted. A collage technique works well. Numbers should label each illustration. Each definition is numbered and copied in the blanks.

The finished visual dictionaries make an attractive classroom display. When they follow a dictionary review and are completed at home, they do not represent a large expenditure of class time, yet they illustrate one of the complexities of language.

Variation: Students number off by sixes, and all form groups by number. Assign each group one of the words below:

1. chair	3. dog	5. gum
2. deck	4. glass	6. suit

One member in each group should be a secretary to write down responses on scratch paper. The task is for each group to think of all the definitions for its word without using a dictionary. After about ten minutes, students should exchange their words and definitions so each group has a different word. After a quick review to see if the groups can add any additional definitions, students should get out their dictionaries. Each group should have more than one kind of dictionary. As many additional definitions as possible should be found.

Explain that the number of definitions (or meanings) for a single word makes English an interesting, though complicated, language. To illustrate this further, offer the visual dictionary assignment as homework or as an extra credit option.

Word Beads

Objective: to foster wider interest in words

Materials: duplicated sheet with word beads and directions —
some blank and some with letters filled in on the
beads (Model Spirit Master 1)

Procedure: Devices, puzzles, and games that provide opportunities for students to work with words are valuable classroom additions. Word beads are letter chains that offer students practice in a different kind of word recognition. The idea is for a student to begin at the starting letter and list every word she finds within the bead chain using the letters in order. She can consult a dictionary to check spelling. As soon as she has found all the words beginning with the first letter, she moves to the next letter to list the words that begin there. She repeats this until she has worked all the way around the chain.

On the next page is a sample word-bead sheet filled in with letters. No special order is required, so that every sheet can be filled in randomly with letters, making each one different. The approximate number of possible words should be given on every sheet.

A blank sheet for duplication can be made by tracing around a dime until a bead chain is completed. The rules are typed in the center before the chain is duplicated. A numbered classroom set can be made by filling in several sheets differently. Thus, an answer key could be easily coded to the numbers and/or students could easily keep track of which sheets they had tried by recording the numbers. Since so many of the words are quite short and easy, this is a word game that offers lower-ability students a chance for success.

Model Spirit Master 1
Word-Bead Sheet

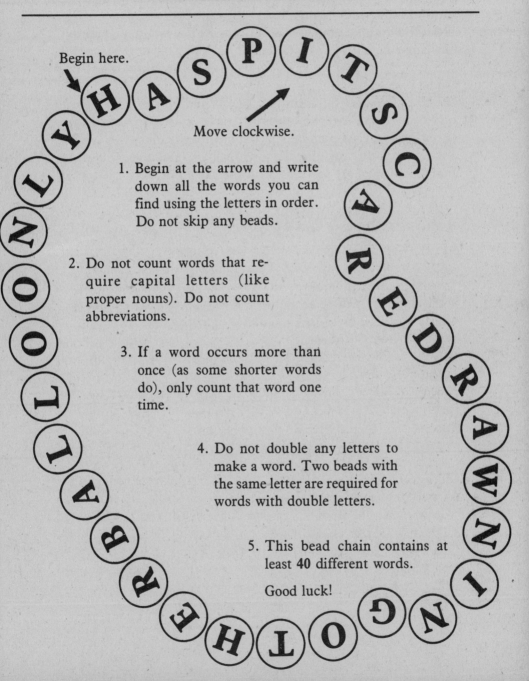

Begin here.

Move clockwise.

1. Begin at the arrow and write down all the words you can find using the letters in order. Do not skip any beads.

2. Do not count words that require capital letters (like proper nouns). Do not count abbreviations.

3. If a word occurs more than once (as some shorter words do), only count that word one time.

4. Do not double any letters to make a word. Two beads with the same letter are required for words with double letters.

5. This bead chain contains at least **40** different words.

Good luck!

Variation: Perhaps the variation will actually prove the better learning experience. Have extra blank sheets available with just the unfilled beads and the directions on them. Invite students to take these and create their own word beads. If you want competition, challenge them to see who can make the string of word beads with the greatest number of possible words. You might request that students also provide their own answer keys. This requires them to check dictionaries for legitimate words and correct spellings. A quick way to evaluate the sheets is to have students exchange their sheets among class members to see how well students match the answer keys. By providing the sheets with blank beads, you insure that all students are working with the same number of letters.

Answers to sample word beads:

ha	it	redrawn	he
has	its	draw	her
hasp	scar	drawn	herb
a	scare	raw	herbal
as	scared	awning	ball
asp	car	in	balloon
spit	care	ingot	all
spits	cared	go	lo
pi	are	got	loon
pit	red	other	on
pits	redraw	the	only

An Affixing Race

Objective: to demonstrate the adaptability of words through the process of affixing

to introduce or conclude a study of prefixes and suffixes

Materials: dictionaries, one per student if possible

Procedure: Most students are unaware of the variety of changes a root word undergoes with the addition of prefixes or suffixes. To introduce the concept, brainstorm with a class, asking them to think of all the prefixes and suffixes they know. As each one is called out, ask if it is a prefix or suffix. Write all the prefixes on one side of the chalkboard and all the suffixes on the other.

After the students have run out of ideas, divide them into about five groups. Assign each group a root word and the task to make as many words as possible by adding prefixes and suffixes to the root. They may add any legitimate combinations as long as the resulting word is an acceptable English word. Since each group has a different root word, there is really no competition to the activity. However, setting a limit on the length of time students can work makes the activity seem like a game or a race. It becomes a race where everyone can win because the group that only comes up with 11 words can claim they had a harder word than the group that found 32 — which might be true.

Some possible root words for the five groups are:

know
claim
spell
store
appoint

Students who had not thought of *ment* as a suffix earlier during the class brainstorming session will think of it when given the word *appoint*. Some will have missed the common little *s* to make plural forms but will find it during the race. Each group should have at least one secretary to write down words as the others think and consult dictionaries. Questions will arise about things like the *ex* in *exclaim*. Others will be about whether a whole word can be a prefix or a suffix as in *dime*store or spell*bound*. Questions of spelling changes will arise. All of these lead to an understanding of the affixing process.

Sometimes a simple explanation will give students the key to understanding. For example, students should check the etymology of a word like *claim*. Inside the brackets in the dictionary, they will find that the word came from L (Latin) *clamare*, which means *call*. Checking the prefix *ex* will show them it means *out* in Latin. The definition of *exclaim* will show that it means *call out*, and the etymology will reveal that it is from the Latin *exclamare*. This is double proof that it is an affixed word. Usually, either the etymology or the definition will show whether the word is composed of a root and prefix or suffix. Words like *dimestore* and *spellbound* are examples of compounding rather than affixing. The clue is that each part of the word is a word in itself. True, *bound* can be used in some other combinations, but usually it takes affixes (as in *rebound*) rather than provides them. Sometimes the identification of compound words gets a little fuzzy, so it is best not to have a hard and fast rule.

When time is up and students have tallied their totals, go back to the chalkboard and add additional suffixes and prefixes to the original list. This is a good time to formulate a definition for both *prefix* and *suffix*. For example, a prefix is something placed before a word to change or qualify its meaning.

Variation: The idea of taking a root word and, through affixing, making as many different words as possible can be used on an individual basis also. Individual students each do the same word or opt to find their own words. If a student chooses his own word, he might accidentally select one without too many possibilities although the teacher should recognize this and not penalize him if he has only a few words. The individual search works well as a homework assignment or an extra credit option.

Although there are no answer keys for activities like these, they are not hard to check. A quick reading will show the non-words. A questionable word might require a quick dictionary check. There are fewer chances for invention in giving the root word than in giving just the prefix or suffix. A student could go wild, for example, making words with *un*. Although this is called a race, winning isn't important; trying is.

What Is My Abode?

Objective: to introduce or review the thesaurus

Materials: a dictionary, several copies of the thesaurus duplicated sheets with word search, one per student   (Model Spirit Master 2)

Procedure: If students are not already familiar with a thesaurus, introduce them to this useful writing tool. To do this, write the title of this chapter on the blackboard. Ask students if anyone can answer the question. Students may be unsure of the meaning of *abode*. Allow a student to look up the word in a dictionary if no one is positive of its meaning. The dictionary may throw students a curve by giving students a synonym like *habitation*. A simpler dictionary will likely give *dwelling, place,* or maybe even *home*.

Once students understand the meaning of *abode*, they can begin to answer the question. Write each different answer on the board. Ask students to think of synonyms for places where humans dwell. Keep adding new contributions to the list. When all ideas seem to be exhausted, explain that there is a book that contains just what they have made — a list of synonyms for a word.

If there isn't a whole class set of the thesaurus, distribute as many as are available among the students. Together, study the organization, perhaps looking up a common word like *boy* or *girl*. As students discover unusual synonyms like *wench*, point out that synonyms have shades of meaning that are not always exact matches. Thus, students must use caution in choosing a synonym.

Checking the entry for *abode* will reveal many additional words not on their list. It is unlikely that anyone has contributed *casa* or *kiosk*, for example. Therefore, a student would never arbitrarily select to use *kiosk* as a synonyms for *house* without checking its meaning in a dictionary.

Looking up *abode* will indicate another aspect of a thesaurus. Point out that the words are grouped by their part of speech. When replacing a noun, a student must be sure to find the noun synonyms. Note also that certain slang words and phrases are included. Mention that entry words are limited too. Not every word that appears in a dictionary is included in a thesaurus. Have students analyze entries to see what is included.

A follow-up activity could be a word search based on a thesaurus entry like the one on the following page. With really sharp students, eliminate the list of included words from the bottom. Instead, let a student work with a thesaurus only, circling each synonym as she finds it and keeping her own list of the words in the search. Obviously, the student with the most complete list of synonyms will be the one who has done the best. Doing a word search without a list of words is a real challenge.

Variation: Instead of duplicating a word search, invite students to create their own for a thesaurus entry. No size limit need be set, but advise against anything larger than twenty letters by twenty. Otherwise, students will leave too many unused letters that just fill space. Creating a word search could be an extra credit activity.

Model Spirit Master 2
Thesaurus Word Search

```
R K T E N E M E N T E C N E D I S E R H
A D C O N D O M I N I U M H L L A H U F
N T U A T I A D N E I C A H M Z S T R A
C O E P B Z H C J L A J N S O R A D V R
H W C X L O G C A B I N S V T V C U I M
H N H S T E D C P S Z Y I C E N E G L H
O H A E E T X E A D T K O R L H L L L O
U O L Y V W H L R W E L N I H O U U A U
S U E U A H S L T E N T E H O U S E E S
E S T G C I B V M L P W T B M S Y H N E
H E R M I T A G E L O M I K E E R I O K
P A L A C E C H N I S V A G R B O T T B
E L E T R H P U T N R H L C W O T E S A
N I L J C O T T A G E E A L L A I N N R
T S N E L U N R L H T B K N E T M T W R
H H C N C S C A F O I O I Z T C R S O A
O H O S T E L I M N O T O N F Y O V R C
U M C U H A L L O L E A S Y N I D K B K
S H A C K U T E G D O L K A D O B E L S
E S T A T E A R K R H F B U N G A L O W
```

ABODE	CONDOMINIUM	HOUSE	RANCH HOUSE
ADOBE	COTTAGE	HOUSEBOAT	RESIDENCE
APARTMENT	DORMITORY	HOVEL	SHACK
ARK (2)	DUPLEX	HUT (2)	SHANTY
BARRACKS	DWELLING	IGLOO	TAVERN
BROWNSTONE	ESTATE	INN (2)	TENEMENT
BUNGALOW	FARMHOUSE	KIOSK	TENT (2)
CABIN	FLAT (2)	LODGE	TOWNHOUSE
CAMPER	HACIENDA	LOG CABIN	TRAILER
CASA	HALL (2)	MANOR	VILLA
CASTLE	HERMITAGE	MANSION	WHITEHOUSE
CAVE	HOME	MOTEL (2)	WIGWAM
CELL (2)	HOSTEL	PALACE	
CHALET	HOTEL	PENTHOUSE	

(Numbers indicate words that occur twice.)

Alive And Well And Hiding
In English

Objective: to demonstrate how foreign words are absorbed into other languages

Materials: pattern tree and leaf   (Model Spirit Master 3)
dictionaries that give etymologies for words

Procedure: If students will accept that one of the definitions of a living thing is that it grows and changes, they will understand why all modern, spoken languages are considered living. New words are added continuously; old usages slip into obscurity. This is true of all spoken languages, but not really true of Latin. Yet Latin isn't as dead as it could be either. True, there are no new Latin words being added, but Latin stem words, prefixes, and suffixes are still incorporated in many modern languages. French and Spanish and the other Romance languages are closely linked to their Latin ancestor, but so is English, although it is considered a Germanic language. Many English words evolved from the Norman French and carry Latin roots. Tracing certain modern words to their Latin origins demonstrates that Latin is not really dead. It lives, though hidden, in many English descendants.

This can be illustrated in a challenging group project. Divide the class into six groups and assign each a different root or stem from Latin. The following are good roots for this project:

porto (meaning carry)   spect (meaning look)
tract (meaning draw, pull) pend (meaning hang)
dico (meaning speak, say)   voc, vok (meaning call)

Each group should have a secretary to record all the words that evolved from the Latin root. Each group should have several dictionaries containing etymological information. Caution the group that in checking the etymology for the right root, there may be variations in the spellings of the root, depending on which form of the word was used. However, even if the spelling is not identical, it should be accepted if it came from a similar Latin root with the same meaning. Usually the etymology states what the meaning of the root is.

All these words should be collected by the secretary and correctly spelled. The easiest way to begin is by looking up English words that start with the same letters. If the meaning seems related to the Latin meaning, check the etymology. Each different form of the word is accepted as a separate word. Thus, both *portage* and *portable* would count as separate words, and *portability* would be considered a third word. Students should check that the word is from the right root.

It may be harder for students to find words in which the Latin root appears in the middle or at the end. It might be necessary to supply each group with one word to get them started. For example:

transport	inspect
extract	suspension
predict	revoke

Students can then begin experimenting by trying various prefixes with their roots and then checking the dictionary.

As the words are collected, they should be transferred to leaf shapes cut from green paper. Basically, the leaves should be long and narrow to allow words to be written on them. The leaf might be similar to 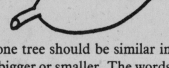 the shape at the right. All leaves on one tree should be similar in shape, though some could be slightly bigger or smaller. The words should be clearly and neatly printed or written so that they can be easily read. Don't rush; this activity will take more than one day.

The finished leaves should be glued to an outline of a tree similar to the one on the next page. They need only a dot of glue at the stem end of the leaf and should be attached to a branch on the tree, anywhere a leaf would normally grow. In the box in the root section, the Latin root and its meaning should be written. Since all of these roots have many English descendants, the tree should be flourishing with green leaves. Since each word contains a bit of Latin, it can be said that the language is still alive and well and hiding in English.

Variation: A student who works quickly might undertake this same activity on an individual basis. Working alone in spare class-time, it might take several days to complete, so no time limit should be set.

Model Spirit Master 3
Word Tree Pattern

26

Illustrating Idioms

Objective: to enjoy one of language's most curious constructions

Materials: pack of 4″ x 6″ index cards

Procedure: Because idioms add such color to a language, they are fun to study. Every language has its idioms, but they differ from language to language. What makes them interesting is that their meanings are entirely different from what their words actually say. Native speakers usually pick up on these simply by hearing them used, but foreign speakers are utterly confused. Because every language has its idioms, books for teaching any language usually contain a table of common idioms.

Most native speakers are unaware how many idioms they know and use. To demonstrate this, have the class brainstorm idioms they know. Write them on the board as fast as students call them out. It may be necessary to prime them a bit by asking a question like, "What does it mean to turn over a new leaf?" Another might be, "How would you know if your mother blew her top?" Obviously, the literal meaning is incorrect. You do not seek fresh, green vegetation and flip it underside up or set a charge of explosives to the head. Because the meanings of these word groups are completely different, they are idioms. Students will begin to contribute their own quickly. At first, it may be best just to get them all written down, although later their actual meanings should be discussed. Books that explain the origins of many idioms may be fun to share with the class.

In no time, a list far more comprehensive than the following should fill the chalkboard:

don't put your eggs all in one basket
how time flies

27

in the soup
having a green thumb
on pins and needles
make the fur fly
button your mouth
burning the midnight oil
like a fish out of water
raise the roof
the cat's got your tongue
drinks are on the house
apple polishing
that's the way the cookie crumbles
in hot water
don't go spinning your wheels
be on cloud nine

Brainstorming with the class will produce a long list of idioms. However, a carry-over assignment asking students to collect idioms from their parents or friends will expand the list even more. A bulletin board might even be set aside for a few weeks and covered with bright paper. Using felt-tipped markers, you can cover the board with idioms as students contribute them.

Because so many idioms have such a sharp visual image, students who enjoy drawing will enjoy illustrating idioms on the unlined sides of the index cards. Since not everyone can draw, this sort of activity should not be assigned, required, or graded. It can be an optional choice from a list of vocabulary projects within a unit of word study. If there are enough illustrated idioms, they might fill a bulletin board by themselves. Otherwise, they can be scattered across a bulletin board with other idioms written but not illustrated.

Another variation to idiom study is to collect the idioms in a spiral notebook instead of on a bulletin board. The index card illustrations are glued in to illustrate various pages. A book of idioms is more lasting than a two-week bulletin board in a classroom. Students can also make their own individual books or keep a separate page or two in their English books. The important thing is that students recognize idioms and are aware of their use.

Variation: If there is a non-English speaking student in the school, make a book of idioms in dictionary form for him. Group or alphabetize the idioms and write clear English definitions for each. If there are special classrooms for non-English speaking students within your school system, two or three copies of an idiom dictionary can be made to donate to such classrooms.

Some students might enjoy writing an imaginary telephone conversation between two speakers who rely heavily on idioms. For example:

> JOE: Hi, Ted! What's cooking?
> TED: Man, the whole place is jumping.
> JOE: Really? What's the scoop?
> TED: Well, my Uncle Louie flew the coop. (etc.)

Such an activity demonstrates the slangy quality of idioms and how their overuse destroys precision in speech or writing.

Composition Collection

I feel a deep commitment to teach students to write skillfully. I agree that much of the creative art cannot be taught, but I believe the mechanical aspects can be. Although inspiration is essential, much of writing is a learned skill — practiced and polished. The lessons in this section basically offer practice — in organizing a paragraph, in being aware of modifying structures, in patterning after models, and in finishing stories. Opportunities to polish are offered in the chance to use figurative language, to develop a theme, and to handle the three elements of a short story — plot, character, and setting. Of course, these do not represent a total composition program, but used with your existing lessons, I hope they broaden your students' writing experiences.

Models For Success

Objective: to insure a successful, one-paragraph composition
to provide practice in paragraph organization

Materials: copies of model paragraphs (Model Spirit Masters 4 and 5)

Procedure: Mention of a writing assignment brings instant despair to some students. These are the ones who feel they have nothing to say or, from markings on previous papers, know they aren't working well with sentence structure. Some might have been told their papers lack organization. Still others just feel inadequate to a writing task. For these students, a writing assignment is just one more opportunity for failure. Obviously, these students need a successful writing experience more than any of the others.

To insure some success, any teacher can build a model paragraph frame that students begin with. Each student fills in the blanks with specific details from his own life and experiences. The trick is to build the model on such a universal theme that all students can relate to it. Nearly every child has at some time been smitten with some animal, from a baby bird fallen from its nest to a champion show dog. Most people mentally plan some ideal dream vacation. Using these two experiences as raw materials, the paragraph models on the following pages evolved.

A sheet with a model paragraph can be passed to every student in a class or used prescriptively by only those who need it. Even more able students can profit from completing a model because it offers more sophistication in sentence structure and more variety in sentence openings than average students use on their own. The blank-filling offers chances to work at using specific details and sharp wording. If, however, the class includes some students who are already gifted writers, a simple model like the following ones might be too easy for them. For gifted writers, a truly challenging model would have to be designed if the assignment is used with them. A possibility for these students might be actual prose paragraphs from distinguished writers with details and specifics omitted. Otherwise, there is some value in having a whole class work on a model together.

If there are sufficient copies of the model paragraphs, students may select the one they prefer. They may then write directly on the model rather than use scratch paper. Usually, a student feels less pressured if the finished paper is not due at the end of the class period. With enough copies of the model, students can use the sheets as homework. Such an option does not penalize the slow worker. Most students are pleased with their finished paragraphs. If they keep notebooks of their writings, these model paragraphs make good additions.

Variation: Sample models similar to these can be kept in notebooks at a writing center so students can follow through with them on their own. Also, models for compositions make excellent additions to lap packs. Having them available to students when they need or want them makes them useful for individualized work.

Model Spirit Master 4
Model Paragraph

Study the model paragraph below. Decide what you would put in each of the blanks. Use scratch paper to write out your ideas if you wish.

When you are ready, copy the sentences in order on a clean sheet of paper. Remember to indent the first sentence.

Each numbered group of words should be one sentence. Remember to use a capital at the beginning and a period at the end. Begin sentence #2 right after #1. Do not begin a new line unless there is no more room. Continue with sentence #3 after #2. Do not put the numbers in your paper. They are just to help you keep your place.

Write neatly, and check spellings for any unfamiliar words you add. Turn in your finished paper with your name on it.

An Animal I Loved

1. Perhaps of all the animals I have ever known, I loved

_____ best.
    animal's name

2. _____ was _____ that belonged
    name   *description, kind, color, etc.*

to _____ .
    owner

3. What made _____ special was
                    name

_____ .
    quality or characteristic

4. I first met _____ when _____
   name   *circumstances*

_____ .

5. Very clearly, I remember _____
                              one specific detail of animal

_____ .
   one particular incident

6. We used to _____ .
               something you did together

7. Even when I am old, I think I will remember _____
                                                 name

because _____ .
        reason

Model Spirit Master 5
Model Paragraph

Study the model paragraph below. Decide what you would put in each of the blanks. Use scratch paper to write out your ideas.

When you are ready, copy the sentences in order on a clean sheet of paper. Remember to indent the first sentence.

Each numbered group of words should be one sentence. Remember to use a capital at the beginning and a period at the end. Begin sentence #2 right after #1. Do not begin a new line unless there is no more room. Continue with sentence #3 after #2. Do not put the numbers in your paper. They are just to help you keep your place.

Write neatly, and check spellings for any unfamiliar words you use. Turn in your finished paper with your name on it.

The Ideal Vacation

1. An ideal vacation would be _____ in _____ .

how long   where

2. I would like this because _____ .

reason why

3. The best thing about _____ is _____ .

place   what?

4. If I were there, I would _____ and _____ .

mention activity   second activity

5. On a typical day, I would get up around _____ and
   _____ .

time

do what

6. Later, I would _____ , and at night, I would
   _____ .

do what

what else

7. This, to me, would be _____ .

your feelings

A Circle Of Life

Objective: to offer practice in categorizing
to develop observational skills
to organize a one-paragraph structure

Materials: a 3' — 4' length of string or yarn per student

Procedure: Too many students, when told to write something, genuinely have nothing to say. Another group may have something to say but no idea of how to organize it. These two problems can be met in one version of a familiar assignment. Plus, this assignment carries a bonus as it takes the class outside the classroom.

If possible, save this activity for a clear, warm, dry day, as it works best to take the class outdoors. Each student needs a length of yarn the ends of which are knotted together, pencil or pen, and a notebook or paper on which to take notes. Explain in the classroom that everyone will be going outside to arrange the piece of yarn in a circle somewhere. If there is vegetation around the school, say that the circle should include some living thing. Some student may place her circle on a parking lot that contains an ant, but that does fulfill the requirement. If there is no natural area around the school, the title of the activity can be changed to "A Circle of the City" and should not then require that something living be included. Once draped, the yarn encircles the material for the composition. The student should examine the area carefully and list every single thing she finds. A list might be something like:

> 2 twigs
> some grass
> 11 pebbles
> a candy wrapper
> 4 dandelions, etc.

Although it is fun to get outdoors, the listing only takes a few minutes, and students should be back in the classroom within fifteen minutes. The next step is to make individual lists of items in as many different categories as possible. Categories might be things like the following:

things of nature
things of man
living things
non-living things
plant life
animal life
man-made intentionally (like sidewalk)
man-made carelessly (pollution)
dangerous things (like broken glass), etc.

The categories may overlap at this stage since students won't know just how to organize them. The next step is to review that a paragraph contains a topic sentence, several supporting sentences, and a conclusion. For this particular assignment, the topic sentence will be the first one, and the class may write samples together. A possibility might be: "A four-foot length of yarn can encircle a..." The ending should be general enough to include any possible combination of categories. An ending could be: "...a variety of things." Another could be: "...a surprising number of things." Allow the negative opening if a student wants to say something like, "A four-foot piece of yarn encloses very little of interest to me." This type of opening will work just as well.

Students should then try to write a supportive sentence for each category of items. A possibility might be something like, "Four kinds of living things were seen—grass, dandelions, several ants, and a beetle." Suggest that students work for a natural order—perhaps mentioning things of nature first and then switching to evidence of man, or building from least to greatest, etc. You might mention some possible transition structures like, "In addition," or "Near the middle," or "Also." This will remove the danger of having too many sentences begin: "There were...."

The easiest conclusion is a slight restatement of either the title or the topic sentence. If there has been strong evidence of man's negative influence, another good ending would be a rhetorical question asking how man could do this. Another possible ending is a personal reference indicating what the writer thought or felt.

Depending on how much importance is placed on this assignment, the papers might be required in ink, correctly spelled, etc. Around the perimeter of the writing, the student could glue down a length of her yarn so that her paragraph is encircled. Such finished paragraphs are interesting to display in the classroom.

Variation: If weather or school prohibits going outside, the same activity can be carried on within the school. Various areas are open to brief invasions by students who drop their yarn, make their notes, and leave. Such areas would include: hallways, the library, various offices, the classroom itself, a display case, a particularly scuffed desk or table top, a student's own locker, the wastebasket, etc.

Another variation would be to have students place the yarn somewhere at home and come to class with the list of notes ready.

Mastering Modification

Objective: to provide practice working with modifiers
to demonstrate the importance of structures of modification

Materials: copies of the three paragraphs (Model Spirit Master 6
and 7, cut apart), one for every two students

Procedure: After class study of adjectives and adverbs as single
words, phrases, and clauses, students need practice using these
modifying structures. Too often, drill has been restricted to finding and identifying them within sentences or adding them to
isolated sentences. A different approach is to ask students to remove them from selections, stripping the writing down to the basic
nouns and verbs.

For this exercise, students should work in pairs—usually with
the closest person. If the class has an odd number of students, one
pair can be expanded to a group of three. Each group has one
paragraph from which the students are to strike out all modifiers. If
a, *an*, *the*, and numbers have been considered adjectives, these
words become the exceptions. All other true modifiers are to be
crossed out. The students may consult any class notes or textbooks,
but one pair must not consult another. When all structures of
modification have been eliminated, one student in each pair should
write a copy of the stripped paragraph to share with the class later.
You might tell the class that more than one pair will be working on
the same paragraph, though neighbors should have different ones.

The success of this activity lies in the careful construction of the
paragraphs. They should be obviously different yet so constructed
that when the modifiers are removed, the basic structures are very
similar. A sample set of paragraphs follows:

Model Spirit Master 6
Three Paragraphs

One cold, dark night, the icy wind blew fiercely against the isolated buildings. The heavy sky was filled with fast-moving clouds. Standing in the shed's protection, I felt lonely and vulnerable. Surely I knew what the change in the weather meant — the coming of winter.

One gentle night, the southern wind blew restlessly through the maple leaves. The August sky was dotted with countless stars. Standing beneath the shadowy trees, I felt peaceful. Happily I knew contentment as I listened to the soft, night sounds.

One noisy, music-filled night, the warm wind blew briskly through the holiday crowds. The velvet sky was glowing from the reflections of hundreds of carnival lights. Standing beside the Ferris wheel, I felt excited. Joyfully I knew what I should do to be a part of the gaiety of the riders whirling above the throng.

When the pairs have finished and made their copies of the stripped-down paragraph, one student should be asked to read his first sentence aloud. It should be: "One night the wind blew." Puzzled looks should appear as the sentence should match everyone's first sentence. You probably won't tell the secret yet, but have the second sentence read instead. It should be: "The sky was." The third sentence will probably be "I felt," although some may have included the participle *standing* as well. Since this is not the kind of activity that is graded, it is possible to pause to review the adjective function of a participle. Only in the last sentence should real differences appear. The three possibilities are:

> "I knew what the change meant — the coming."
> "I knew contentment."
> "I knew what I should do to be a part."

The sentences, stripped of their modifiers, might be written on the chalkboard as they are given. Seeing these bare sentences demonstrates how empty writing is without the richness of modification. To show how different each paragraph was to begin with, a student should read each of the three versions aloud. You might take a moment to discuss the different moods each presented and the differences in time. The importance of prepositional phrases as modifiers should also be noted as well as the adverb clause that ends the second paragraph. Quite obviously the most important fact is that the paragraphs really have no meaning without their modifiers.

Variation: You might want to use the more common approach in which students add modifiers to a paragraph containing blanks. Sample directions and a sample paragraph follow:

Model Spirit Master 7
Blank Paragraph

Add details to the paragraph wherever there are blanks. Use as many words or phrases as you want for each numbered blank. Try to make a mood with your word images. Keep the essential sentence structure as it is. When you are satisfied with your choices, write the entire paragraph on a separate sheet of paper.

The __(1)__ October day changed to __(2)__ evening. A lone figure dressed in __(3)__ walked the __(4)__ sidewalks. *His footsteps sounded __(5)__ as he walked __(6)__. Beside him he noticed __(7)__. The street was __(8)__. He stopped at the corner to __(9)__. Around him the air was __(10)__. He could hear __(11)__. The sky seemed __(12)__. He went on alone seeing __(13)__. His heart was filled with __(14)__ for __(15)__. The air held the __(16)__ smell of __(17)__. This he knew was what made October so __(18)__.

*Although the paragraph uses *he* and other masculine pronouns, you may change them to make the character a *she* if you wish.

This paragraph has a slightly different approach as both modifiers and a few nouns are needed and at least one infinitive [#9]. It also incorporates more sensory images to encourage students to describe with more than just visual details. This type of exercise can also be prescribed for the student who writes in vague generalities.

Unfinished Stories

Objective: to stimulate student writing by providing stories to finish

Materials: copies of each story (See Model Spirit Master 8)

Procedure: There will always be students who, when faced with a writing assignment, just cannot get started. Others will sharpen pencils, get out fresh paper, adjust their positions, and be totally unable to think of any idea about which to write. The idea of giving such students story beginnings is not new. In fact, whole books of stories to finish have been published. The idea is basically sound, but using too many of them or using them too often is likely to result in overkill. One or two proven openers kept handy for emergency situations will prove satisfactory. When everyone but one or two students is writing, they need the stimulation of an unfinished story. Sometimes they may not even use the stories, but the stories will serve to prompt their own original ideas. An unfinished story is also an easy assignment to send home for the absent students to complete on her own. It is the ideal prescription for an idea-starved student.

Beginnings of real short stories can be copied and duplicated, or teachers can write their own and duplicate them. Three possible beginnings are given on the following pages. Nearly any subject can be used as long as it offers students optional possibilities for completing it. The direction in which the student takes the story should be up to her, but you may want to set some requirements on the length.

Model Spirit Master 8
Three Stories To Finish

Unfinished Story #1

It has been a long, busy day at school. Every class has been interesting and active. The school lunch was your favorite and was especially delicious today. You were the high scorer for your team in gym class. The teacher appointed you a group chairman in English because your ideas for the play were so exciting.

Now it is last period, and you are in science class watching a movie on reptiles. Usually science class is interesting, but today you are so tired. The room is dark and warm. The projector hums quietly and steadily at the back of the room. Your eyes begin to droop. You are so tired, so ti-re—

You wake up. Everyone is gone! The school is empty and quiet. Outside the classroom windows, it is dark. You have slept through until late at night. You must get home. But wait! Something is different. You suddenly discover you have been changed into a frog!

Assignment: Write about yourself. How have you changed? How do you feel about it? What can you do? What is your reaction? Finish the story.

Unfinished Story #2

It has been a surprisingly warm day for late winter. Tonight as you prepare for bed, you decide to open the window and push out the storm window to let in some of the mild, fresh air. Almost at once you fall asleep.

During the night something wakens you; you are not sure just what. You lie in the dark a moment and feel a tiny pressure on your face. You reach up and switch on your bed light and cover your eyes against the sudden brightness. There seems to be a slight rustling by your ear, but you are not afraid. There is no threatening feeling in the room.

You open your eyes and adjust to the light. Without turning your head, you roll your eyes to the side. Standing beside your ear on your pillow is a little green man about eight inches tall. As you watch him, he bends over and touches your cheek gently with a soft, little hand.

Assignment: Write what happens next. What do you do? Who or what is the little green creature? How did he get to your room? What is your reaction? Finish the story.

Unfinished Story #3

For several weeks you have noticed some unusual things going on in your home. One night you know you left two pencils, one sharpened and one not, beside your mathematics books when you went to bed. In the morning only the unsharpened pencil was there. The photograph of your family stuck in the frame of your dresser mirror disappeared. One day your mother complained that the new writing pad she left by the telephone was half gone already.

Perhaps the strangest thing has been the way your cat acts. You often look up from reading or watching TV to find the cat staring at you. She follows you constantly, watching you eat your meals, do the dishes, talk on the telephone, wash your hair, everything. The cat is making you so nervous you are not sleeping well at night.

One night as you toss restlessly, you are aware of an unusual sound. The whole family is in bed, yet you hear the typewriter.

You get up and tiptoe to the den. The light is on, and seated at the typewriter is your cat! A stack of notes is beside her which she seems to be copying.

Assignment: What is the cat typing? Whose notes is she using? What do you do? What is your reaction? Finish the story.

———————————————

Variation: Another way to use unfinished stories is to type them on unlined 5″ x 8″ index cards. These can be part of a deck of cards to stimulate student writing. Other composition ideas and pictures can be added on other cards to expand the idea deck. It can be kept in a writing center or in the classroom to be drawn from as ideas are needed.

A copy of an unfinished story can be added to a lap pack as an optional activity. Because it needs little direction from a teacher, an unfinished story is excellent for any student-directed learning situation.

Dear Me

Objective: to practice letter–writing skills by writing to a real person

Materials: nothing special, but staplers and tape should be available

Procedure: After completing a unit on the correct forms for letters, students should put their skills into practice. Most people agree that it is better to write a real letter to a real person as many students object to some of the fake situations. An interesting possibility is to have each student write a letter to himself.

Each student should put the date and whatever form is expected at the top. The greeting should contain his own name. If one of the things you have stressed in a friendly letter is to make the content interesting, each student should do this. It is best to use this activity as close to the beginning of the school year as possible. Suggest that students include some of the following in their contents:

> favorite subjects and teachers
> most interesting new boy/girl
> personal goals to achieve
> favorite current song, TV show, etc.
> best friend/friends
> hardest/easiest subject
> significant personal family news

Explain to students that these letters are going to be read by no one except the person mentioned in the greeting. What's more, these letters (once sealed) will not be read again until the last week of school. Thus, any content predicting the future and any evaluating the present will be most interesting many months later. Encourage students not to share their letters as they write. Letters must be finished shortly before the end of the class period.

For the sake of economy, every student does not need his own envelope. When finished, each student should fold his letter in thirds with the writing to the inside. If he has written on the back of his paper, he must take an extra, clean sheet to use around his letter. The letter should be stapled or taped shut, and each student should write his own name on the outside of his folded letter. All of the letters from the class should be put into one large brown envelope, sealed, and marked for identification. If the school has a safe, it would add a touch of drama to put the brown envelope into the safe until the last week of school.

If possible, the teacher should write a letter when the students do. If more than one class does this activity, the teacher need only write with one class. Each class's letters should be sealed in a separate envelope, though, as it adds interest to be marking and sealing the envelope at the end of the class period.

A high point in the year will be the day when the envelope is broken open and the mail delivered. Unfortunately, any new students who arrive during the year will not be receiving any mail. There are some possible ways of having a general letter of welcome ready, which would explain the earlier class assignment. Another possibility might be to have each new student write a similar letter to himself after his first week at the new school. Such an assignment could be typed on a sheet to give to the new student who would complete the assignment on his own time. These letters could be kept in the teacher's desk as the sealed brown envelopes should not be opened to add extra letters; but the new students' letters would be passed back at the same time.

If a student leaves during the year, ask him to address an envelope to himself at his new address. Keep this until the brown envelope is opened. Put his letter to himself (with a brief note from you) into the pre-addressed envelope he left. He will be surprised and pleased to hear from his teacher at his old school.

Variation: Instead of sealing class letters in one large brown envelope, it is possible to have each student buy a stamp and address an envelope to himself. He should use the school address as the return address. The teacher would keep all these letters in their individual, sealed envelopes and after a few months have passed, begin putting them into the U.S. mail. Use no pattern for who gets mail first, but randomly begin sending the mail home. As everyone enjoys getting mail, the students will be glad to get letters too — even if they wrote them themselves.

Writing By Numbers

Objective: to make students aware of the major elements of a short story — plot, setting, and characters
to provide a writing challenge

Materials: a class set of the Short Story Ingredients sheet (Model Spirit Master 9)
several sheets of mimeograph paper in 3 colors (for the variation)

Procedure: Usually students do not consciously use the major elements of a short story in their own writing, although literature study has probably introduced them to characters, setting, and plot. Discuss that an author can choose any elements she wants to complement or counteract one another. For example, a teenager lost in Wyoming in 1965 would have quite different experiences from one lost in the same place in 1865. Being lost in mid-January would differ from mid-June, just as being lost in a city would differ from a wilderness area. Being lost in a stolen car would provide a different situation from being lost on foot. A blind teenager's experiences would also be different, etc. Thus, the potential of these elements creates the interplay in a story. A student who can handle the elements of a short story will write with greater sophistication.

To provide practice with these elements and to challenge students to work with the various possibilities that certain choices offer, ask them each to get out a sheet of clean paper. Tell them you will provide most of the ingredients, but their assignment will be to write a short story, or at least, begin one.

Ask each student to select any two numbers from *1* through *12* and write them on the top of her paper. Next have each choose a third number from *13* through *20*. The last number should be from *21* through *30*. Each student should have four numbers on the top of her paper. Impress on students that they cannot change the numbers later; they are locked in, so to speak. Ask if any of them remember paint-by-number kits from childhood. The pictures were painted by a simple matching technique. Maybe some students used these kits. While they didn't produce original masterpieces, they were fun to do. Of course, accomplished painters don't use them, but they are fun for beginners. Explain that this writing assignment will work on the same principle. The numbers at the tops of their papers will correspond to the numbers of various items which they must use as ingredients for writing a short story.

Pass to each student a copy of the sheet on the next page or one similar to it. Students will be eager to see what their numbers match. Some will protest that it can't be done or that they must get to change just one, but hold firm. To be challenged (which the project should achieve), students must work with their blind choices. If they protest that real writers get to pick their own, admit it, but remind students they are not real writers—at least, not yet. Besides, real writers would probably try this just for fun as a game.

A short story cannot be completed in a class period, so you will have to decide if you want the stories finished. If so, more time must be allowed or the story assigned as homework due a few days hence. Away from class you lose control of the writing situation, so you may want to collect the papers at the end of the period and pass them out again the next day. You might even be satisfied with just the beginnings if students have done a good job weaving the elements together.

Model Spirit Master 9
SHORT STORY INGREDIENTS SHEET

Match your numbers to the items below and work them all into a short story. More elements and characters can be added, but the four you choose must be used.

Characters are:

1. old Dr. Stein whose medical credentials were lost in WW II

_____

2. 15-year-old Robin whose parents are spending 10 days in Europe

_____

3. D.J. West, motorcycle racer

_____

4. Tracey Stone who has held 11 different jobs in 6 years

_____

5. Miss Grey, 50-year-old, unmarried school teacher

_____

6. Orville, 12-year-old boy genius

Setting is:

13. winter

an isolated farmhouse

_____

14. a severe electrical storm

passenger cabin of a jet liner

_____

15. tourist season

a beautiful resort hotel in Spain

_____

16. Christmas Eve

a cheap, furnished apartment

_____

17. night

a 27-room Victorian mansion

Plot involves:

21. a fortune in rare stamps

_____

22. a fire that totally destroyed a huge warehouse

_____

23. a suspicion of arsenic poisoning

_____

24. a letter lost in the mail for over three years

_____

25. a doctor's report of an incurable disease

_____

26. a stolen pedigreed poodle

_____

7. rich, 84-year-old Alice Brady

_____

8. Gwen DeVine, stage actress and movie and TV star

_____

9. Kelly Ives, famous detective

_____

10 Ed Hall, retired three years and totally alone since his wife died

_____

11. Bert Dunn, TV talk show host

_____

12. Lee Davis, young athlete in training for Olympics

_____

18. hunting season

a cabin in the woods

_____

19. Saturday night

city jail

_____

20. dawn

an empty stretch of desert highway

_____

27. automobile accident involving a sports car and a van

_____

28. a revenge plan for a childhood incident

_____

29. an invitation to a party

_____

30. a new job

Variation: Cut pieces of colored mimeograph paper into small pieces about 2″ × 3″. Have three different colors of paper (although one may be white), and cut enough so there will be one piece of each color for each student. Pass every student one piece of one color, for example, blue. Tell each student to think of a possible character for a short story, write on the paper the name for the character, and add a few words describing the character. Collect all the slips. Pass out the second color and request that students indicate a possible setting, not necessarily for the character they just created. Remind students that setting includes both time and place. Collect the second color and pass out the last pieces. On these indicate that students should provide an idea for a plot, something a story might be about. Some slips might contain single words like *love* or *murder*, but this is all right. Since you have not seen all the slips, you cannot be sure that every one is useable. Therefore, you might want to add a few slips of each type yourself. For example, you might want to add a dog or some other animal to the character slips. Many of the characters on the Short Story Ingredients Sheet were genderless. A few names like that allow students the chance to have the character be either male or female.

Of course, the next step is that the slips are passed out randomly or drawn from a hat. Each student is to have one slip of each color. The assignment is the same—to write a short story incorporating the three elements. Only one character slip is used in this assignment to simplify the procedure. Otherwise, there will be too much confusion over whether the students should have two blue or two pink, etc. As before, students have the option of adding additional characters or details to the elements they must use.

This variation might be more trouble than it's worth. However, if the class is well-controlled, the extra busy-work of passing out and collecting slips works smoothly. Also, a departure like this can sometimes catch the interest of a restless class. There will be a lot more interest in the finished stories if they contain elements contributed by other students. In fact, these stories would lead to a good read-aloud sharing. If you decide that the evaluation might be easier by listening to the stories read aloud, tell students at the beginning. Knowing that no one else has to read the story sometimes frees a student to use bigger words, which she would avoid if it meant checking a dictionary for spelling.

Obviously, these two procedures offer several possibilities. The sheet of items can be used again after some time has elapsed. Students will remember what's coming, but they will not remember which numbers match which items. The slips can be used again also or traded with the slips from a different class. Most important, most students will respond well to this unusual way of getting something to write about, and many will come up with unique and complex stories.

Figuratively Speaking

Objective: to enjoy figurative language
to offer opportunities to use figurative language in writing

Materials: sheets with writing situations, one per student (Model Spirit Master 10)
cards with individual situations (for the variation)

Procedure: If the study of figurative language is limited to finding examples in poetry and other literary forms, students are cheated. They should be offered the chance to build figures of speech and incorporate them in writing. This can be a creative, imaginative experience for them.

If students have not looked for and analyzed figures of speech in literature, some review might be necessary. Personification is perhaps the easiest construction. Explain that any time an inanimate object is treated as if it were a human, that's personification. Usually the thing being personified is further identified as a person by being given a capital letter, especially if the personification is carried over for several paragraphs. For example, "In early November, Winter returned bringing her cloak of snow." Students might enjoy a more lighthearted example: "Pete Pencil was tired of being pushed around. He was worn down from working so hard." Such an example also introduces another language device, the play on words. "Pushed around" and "worn down" have a double meaning. People use these expressions, but in relation to what actually happens when a pencil is used, these phrases have another meaning.

Students will be familiar with word plays from riddles. Every child has learned what is "black and white and read all over." In fact, students will have a few new answers, like a zebra with sunburn. A restaurant menu might state, "Let us make your steak a rare treat." This is a play on the word *rare*. Students should catch the word play if you ask if a ghost uses vanishing cream. You may also want to mention puns.

Usually, however, when figurative language is studied, it consists mainly of similes, metaphors, and sometimes hyperbole. Hyperbole, which is basically exaggeration for humorous purposes, will be best known to students as tall tales, for example, the Paul Bunyan stories. Many comedians use this form of humor.

Most students will understand that similes are comparisons using the words *like*, *as*, and sometimes *that*. *Like* and *as* are by far the most common. The danger with similes is that they become too common, too well-known. Then they are called clichés, and they add no freshness to writing. Caution students to beware of saying the same old thing — she eats like a bird; the place looks like a cyclone hit it; it's as dark as night; etc. Sometimes a strange simile is used for humor. This kind is often the reverse of what is expected. Old-fashioned love songs said that love would last "till the end of time" and other enduring things. To make a reverse simile, think of the opposite of what is expected—a young woman promises to love her hero until her nail polish dries. These can be fun to play with.

A metaphor uses an unstated comparison. Instead of saying something is *like* something else, a metaphor simply states something *is* something else. For example, children are headaches. When the idea is stretched over several sentences or paragraphs, it is called an extended metaphor. For example, the telephone is your friend. It's someone you can call upon. It's a friend so intimate that you feel comfortable with it in your bedroom. It's so helpful that you want it with you in the kitchen. It's so reliable that it's the first one you turn to in an emergency, etc.

These examples are enough to get the student going. He needs the beginning of an idea to start his thinking, since figurative language may be quite new to him. After that, he's on his own. A sheet of sample situations like those on the next page can be duplicated. Although the kind of figurative language for each situation is hinted at, the student should feel free to use any of the types he wishes. He should also have the freedom to reject any of these situations and invent his own.

To get the class started, you might pass out the sheets, read each situation together, and discuss which figure of speech could be used. Students can brainstorm a few possible ideas that might work. The following figures of speech should work with the sample situations, though others might work as well:

cat food commercial = play on words
car model name = metaphor
love song lyric = simile
lost-and-found items = personification
newspaper editorial = extended metaphor
one-liner gags = hyperbole
new perfume ad = simile
news story lead = personification

Probably an assignment like this could not be completed in one class period. It would be a good homework activity. Some students might try to add artwork to advertising copy, put a melody to the song, or even write the whole editorial on cancer. An assignment like this can stimulate a lot of interest.

Model Spirit Master 10
Figurative Language Situations

The following situations will give you a chance to try your hand at using figures of speech. You might be surprised how clever you can be.

You work for an advertising agency that is going to do a television commercial for a new cat food. So far, the product is called "Purr-fection," but you can change the name if you want. Write sample copy for the product.

You are an automobile designer about to introduce an exciting, new model to your line of cars. It is small, fast, sporty, economical, but expensive originally. What will you call it? Plan how you will advertise it in a magazine campaign.

You have been a songwriter for seven years. You have just been asked to write an extra love song for a Broadway show. It is to be a song telling what love is like. Come up with about a dozen ideas. (Can you put them in rhyme?)

You run the lost-and-found for a large school, and items are really stacking up for you. You decide to write some notices for the school bulletin as if various lost items were talking and asking to be reclaimed. What might each of the following say:

> A. one tennis shoe
> B. a pair of glasses
> C. an umbrella
> D. an empty purse
> E. a book [say what kind]
> F. any likely lost item

On the newspaper where you work, you have been asked to write an editorial on the dangers of pollution. You use a metaphor in the title of your editorial: "Pollution: The Cancer of Our Environment." How can you extend the metaphor into the editorial itself. Write sample sentences you could use.

You are employed by several comics to write gags for them. One of them just asked you for several one-liners to complete the following beginnings:

> "Her cooking is so bad that...."
> "That car looks like...."
> "My hometown is so small that...."
> "A date with her/him is as exciting as...."
> "The students tried as hard as...."

Your company has developed a new perfume you hope to market in leading teen magazines. You need a name for the fragrance that will appeal to young women and teenagers. You also need a catchy phrase to make it sell. Try to persuade the reader to try it, with clever similes telling the wearer what she will feel like when wearing it. Submit ideas for possible advertising copy.

You write leads for news stories for a television newscast. Today's major story is about a devastating storm that caused millions of dollars of damage and injured dozens of people. Your boss wants a lead describing it as Nature on the warpath. Write it.

Variation: Do the same assignment, except have the sample situations written on 3″ x 5″ (or 4″ x 6″) cards, one sample per card. Make four copies of each card plus add four cards with a message like the following:

> Wild Card! Invent your own situation to use figurative language. The choice is yours.

Shuffle all the cards together and have each student draw one from the pack. You can decide if you will allow a student to trade his card or draw a second time. Usually, the idea of having to write on any example he picks adds just enough challenge to give the assignment some zip. If students are allowed to trade or draw again, the assignment isn't essentially different from having all the sample choices on a duplicated sheet.

Miscellaneous Mix

I know I need variety in my own teaching to keep me from getting stale, so I assume my students will do better with a little variety in their learning diet as well. The lessons in this section add the spice to the year. You will notice most of them are tied to real skills, though some are really more like play than work. I justify a lesson now and then that has game qualities because it builds class rapport and students' enthusiasm. Mastering spelling, classifying, and improving perception are all touched on in this section, but not treated heavily. Sometimes the lesson offers just another way to think about things, but thinking should be encouraged in all its aspects. At the last evaluation, I want my students to remember that they learned in my classes and had some good times while they did.

Words In Pictures

Objective: to create interest in words

Materials: copies of the pictured words sheet, one per student (Model Spirit Master 11)

Procedure: During the course of a year, students will often work, directly and indirectly, expanding their vocabularies. To generate their interest in words, it is sometimes helpful to use a just-for-fun activity. This can be used at the beginning of the year when students are still rather stiff and self-conscious. It can serve as an ice-breaker and a positive introduction to further vocabulary study. Used during the year, it can inject a pleasant change of pace and pique a renewed interest in word study.

Prepare a sheet of word, phrase, and sentence messages similar to the sample in this chapter. Duplicate it so that there is a copy for each student or each pair of students. Slower classes might work more comfortably in groups of two or three. Since the sheets are not written on, one set can be used many times.

To introduce the sheet, you might say that each box contains a well-known phrase or term or a sentence, but that the message is partly hidden in each. For example, put this box on the chalkboard:

If no one recognizes that the term is "upside down cake," give the answer. Pass out the sheets and perhaps do one or two together. Stress that each box must be considered as a separate unit.

Model Spirit Master 11

1 DON'T eat.	**2** (image of oil with oi and tall i)	**3** i p / m u / x	**4** stand **I**	**5** reading / reading / reading / reading
6 Engalish	**7** GROUND / feet feet / feet feet / feet feet	**8** (dashed circle)	**9** R O A D S / R O A D S	**10** sand (cube)
11 cheaper cheaper / cheaper cheaper / cheaper cheaper / cheaper cheaper / cheaper cheaper / cheaper cheaper	**12** —— flight	**13** once 5PM	**14** PRICE	**15** mind matter
16 DICE DICE	**17** wear long	**18** LIVING	**19** LE VEL	**20** you j u s t me
21 GI / CCCC / CCC	**22** BLOUSE (curved)	**23** DECI SION	**24** ecnalg	**25** (reclining figure)
26 season	**27** PROFILE	**28** c a n d y (in box)	**29** O / B.S. / Ph.D. / D.D.S.	**30** kick
31 DIS / CUS / SION	**32** SLOW	**33** education	**34** (figure)	**35** HEART

Some students will already know some of these or others close enough so that they can solve them quickly. Some squares may have more than one good answer. To avoid confusion and keep everyone from calling answers out loud, it might be wise to have students number a scratch paper and record their answers, one sheet per student or group.

Possible answers to the sample squares are:

1. Don't overeat.
2. eye shadow
3. mix-up
4. I understand.
5. reading between the lines
6. an *A* in English
7. six feet under ground
8. dashing around
9. crossroads
10. sandbox
11. cheaper by the dozen
12. space flight
13. Once upon a time
14. half-price
15. mind over matter
16. paradise
17. long underwear
18. high living
19. split level or bi-level
20. just between you and me
21. G I overseas
22. see-through blouse
23. split decision
24. backward glance
25. laying it on the line
26. fruit in season
27. low profile
28. candy bar
29. three degrees below zero
30. sidekick
31. open discussion
32. slow-up
33. board of education
34. a hole in one
35. a broken heart

After a reasonable time or on the next day, correct answers can be shared. When students are stumped, the teacher can give the suggested response. Obviously, such an activity would not be scored or graded. Encourage students to look at words more closely and visualize their language. For the next few days students may bring in similar examples to put on the chalkboard and challenge the class.

Variation: Use a similar sheet as a bonus—to those who finish a test early, as a gift the day before Christmas vacation, etc.

The problems can be drawn on 9" x 9" squares of colored construction paper and put up on the bulletin board one at a time. Each day would offer a new puzzle and give the answer to the previous day's square. Students could contribute their ideas, and the set could last many weeks.

Rhyme Words

Objective: to provide additional practice in recognizing variant spellings for common sounds in English words

Materials: 23 small cards (about 1″ × 2″)
one white envelope

Procedure: Many students have trouble with the variations in spelling for the same sounds in English words. It is sometimes helpful to have an extra practice handy that a student can work through individually at her own pace. A good method is to make the practice similar to a game. To do this, cut unlined index cards into pieces about 1″ × 2″. These will serve as the "game" pieces and can be kept in a handy envelope bearing the instructions.

Write one word to a card. Eleven of the words should have a rhyme word that has a different spelling for the rhymed sound. Write these 11 rhyme matches on separate cards. One extra word is added that will not rhyme with any of the other words but that looks visually as though it might. This extra word is put in to discourage guessing. Once the cards are prepared, they can be covered with clear acetate film to give them longer life.

Care must be taken in selecting the rhyme words. *School* and *cool* cannot be used, since they have the same spelling for the rhymed sound. The set should not include a series like *flea, key, see,* and *he,* since they all rhyme with each other so that there is no one correct match for any one of the words. The following words make a good set:

1. cough	7. dough	13. ooze	19. maize
2. off	8. flow	14. lose	20. days
3. half	9. boot	15. cow	21. cool
4. laugh	10. chute	16. bough	22. rule
5. guy	11. doze	17. sea	23. rough
6. sky	12. rose	18. key	

The envelope should contain directions similar to those printed below, so that a student can pursue the activity on her own:

Lay out the cards in this envelope. Put them together to form pairs that rhyme. There will be one extra word that has no rhyme.

Use the pronunciation in parentheses ( ) in the dictionary for any words you do not know.

When all the pairs have been matched, number a piece of your paper from 1 to 11. Copy down a pair for each number in any order.

When you have finished, put the word cards in this envelope. Give the envelope to the teacher along with your finished paper. The teacher will check your work.

The teacher can quickly check the answers, or an answer card can be made for the student to check her own work. An exercise like this can be included as part of a lap pack or used separately as a skill builder whenever a student has free time.

Variation: This activity can be written up and duplicated for a class activity. However, a student does not then have the loose cards to arrange. Manipulating the cards and rearranging the pairs does help some students think better. Also, having the whole class do the exercise together builds in a sense of competition to see who finishes first or who gets the most pairs correct. The need to hurry might lead to careless errors, which would not surface if the student was working alone at her own pace. The student who needs this kind of practice does not need to compete with those who have variant spelling problems pretty well mastered.

A better variation would be to convert the cards to a game for several students to use together. To do this, don't write on the backs of the cards. One of the rhymed words from each pair requires some mark on its back—perhaps a gold star or a sticker. The cards so marked are placed facedown on a table. Students place the other 11 rhyming words and the extra word faceup. The first student draws one of the marked cards and tries to match it with those lying faceup. If she is successful, she keeps the pair and draws a second word to try again. She keeps the cards again if she is successful, but play passes to her left as no one has more than two tries per turn. If the student had made an incorrect match, the marked card is again placed facedown with the others, and the player loses her turn. The bonus try is only after a correct match. At the end of the game, the player with the most cards is the winner. An odd number like 11 just about eliminates any chance of ties. An extra student should sit with the players and hold the answer card. She then determines which pairs are accepted or rejected, but she cannot play. After one round, the card holder can be the winner of the previous game. Thus, those who need the most practice get to play most often.

If this exercise meets a satisfactory response, the teacher can easily make a second or third set of cards using different sounds or different spellings for these same sounds. This same idea can also be used to provide practice in recognizing variant spellings in beginning sounds. For example, words like *kick* and *cane* would make a match. However, this eliminates the element of rhyme in the exercise. Rhyme is not really necessary, but it does add an extra interest to the practice.

Book Report Collages

Objective: to offer another approach to the traditional book report

Materials: old magazines to cut up

Procedure: It is always a good idea to encourage reading. And, it's also important to check students' reading in some way. Yet sometimes it is nearly impossible to enjoy book reports. Students lack the imagination to write zesty reports. Teachers lack the time to read the stacks of papers. The result is that almost everyone dislikes book reports.

Of course, there are some interesting types of book reports like fake diaries and letters or acting scripts for favorite scenes. Even so, the paperwork builds up. The next solution is the oral book report, which is evaluated as it is given. This saves teacher-time later, but it can mean some deadly class sessions as poor speaker follows poor speaker with little to say and less that's remembered. The reasonable solution seems to be to make the oral reports more interesting. Book collages can do this.

If students do not understand that a collage is assembled from many pictures and words cut into interesting shapes and glued to a flat surface, it might be necessary to show several examples. All of the pictures and words have a relationship to each other in a good collage. When the collage is an attempt to interpret or represent a book, the relationship is vital. Even the background shape to which the elements are glued can be integrated into the message. A book dealing with winning at tennis could have words and pictures glued to the cut-out shape of a trophy cup. The story of a Florida adventure might be represented against the cut-out shape of the state of Florida. Although largely composed of words and pictures, some lightweight, three-dimensional items can also be attached. Color always adds interest, as do small sections of shiny gold and silver paper. Even the shape to which everything is glued can add to the meaning. The shape can be rolled up into a tube, folded, strung on a mobile, etc. The design and execution are flexible.

The assignment is to make a collage to represent the book. Later, the collage will be shared with the class through a brief explanation. The presentation is the oral report in disguise. Students may work in class, cutting out pictures and words if time is available. Perhaps a stack of old magazines can be kept available for use when some students finish their work early or to use in study periods. The final assembly is best done at home, as gluing and pasting can get pretty messy. Also, too many loose, little pieces around the classroom can get lost or swept away easily. Some students may want to use paint. Some will work quickly while others will stretch the project out. They can decide on their own time.

The finished reports are shared with the class as an explanation of what was glued on and why. Some students may have drawn some of the pictures themselves, a talent they might have kept hidden. Even the shyest has something to say. An incidental bonus is that many students unconsciously use symbolism. After a few statements like, "I used this to represent...," you can give an impromptu lesson on symbolism in literature. A few will even recognize the intended symbolism in their books and will mention it as shown in the collage. The class will have something to look at during the reports that will help hold their interest. Some will even request that a collage or two be passed around for closer inspection. The speaker has something to talk about and something to do with his hands—holding the collage and pointing to various parts. The teacher has no extra papers to correct. The completed collages make excellent bulletin board materials. All in all, the book report in collage form is a positive experience for everyone.

Variation: The collage representation can work just as well as a project for a short story. It also makes a good choice as one possible project in a unit that offers several choices.

Sometimes small groups of students all read the same book. An interesting way for a whole group to report is to make a collage mobile as their final project. One shape on the mobile could represent each of the main characters, for example. Various students could be responsible for separate parts, but the finished mobile would be a group effort.

Classifying

Objective: to help students recognize common characteristics
to refine ability to categorize

Materials: sheets containing the 20 items, one per student or one per pair (Model Spirit Master 12)

Procedure: The key to mastering systems of classification is recognizing similarities and differences. If students can examine any set of items and recognize what traits the items have in common, they can recognize the category and label it. On the chalkboard, place a series like the following:

> Miami Dolphins
> Chicago Bears
> Oakland Raiders
> Fighting Irish
> New York Jets

Asking students to indicate what these groups have in common will elicit the response that they are all football teams. This is the label for this particular category. To refine their thinking, ask which of the teams is somewhat different from the other four. They should point out that the Fighting Irish is from Notre Dame, a college team. If that one item were removed from the group, the remaining items could be drawn into a tighter grouping with a more specific label. The students should see that the new group could be correctly identified as *professional* football teams. Removing the slightly different item and making a tighter, more exact category requires a higher degree of sophistication than just identifying general categories. This exercise offers that practice.

Although students can work alone, there are certain advantages in working with a partner. Each can question and challenge the thinking of the other as they search for categories. One student from each pair should prepare an answer sheet. A clean sheet of paper should be folded into three columns and the lines numbered from 1 to 20 down the lefthand side. The first column should be labeled "General Category." The middle column should be "Item To Remove," while the last one is "Specific Sub-category." By writing on separate paper, the duplicated sheets can be used again with other classes. Students should be told that their task is to do the same kind of classifying as they did with the items on the chalkboard. They may skip any items that appear too difficult, but they should be aware that some groups might have more than one possible correct solution.

Pass out duplicated sheets of items like the one on the next page, or create your own. If there are enough, each student can have a sheet. Otherwise, one student has the classifying sheet while the other has the answer sheet to fill in. Both students' names should be on the one answer sheet. At the end of the period, students may exchange papers to correct them or correct their own. This type of activity is usually not graded, but the teacher should collect the answer sheets to look over for a hasty check of individual effort.

The teacher who makes her own sheet of items to classify will probably have items more relevant to her students and their interests. However, care is necessary in composing the items. If the list is intended for the file to be used another year, care must be taken not to make the items too topical. This year's economic crisis may not be next year's. The National League pitcher this year could be in the American League next. Songs popular this year won't be next year. To insure success and minimize frustration, the sheet must contain categories easy enough to encourage and others obscure enough to challenge. Also, the teacher must accept any correct answers.

Model Spirit Master 12
Classification Categories Sheet

Sample sheet of items to classify:

Classifying

Each numbered group represents a general category. Identify each and put the correct label on your answer sheet. One item should be removed and written on your answer sheet in the second column. Identify the remaining, specific category in the third column.

Example: apple, pear, potato, peach, banana
Answers: foods   potato   fruits

1. spruce, oak, maple, sycamore, birch
2. Civil War, Revolutionary War, Boer War, Spanish-American War, World War I
3. cotton, rayon, silk, linen, wool
4. Illinois, Nevada, Hawaii, Georgia, Kansas
5. pecan, hickory, walnut, almond, peanut
6. Cadillac, Volvo, Ford, Dodge, Chevrolet
7. Piper Cub, 747, glider, DC-10, fighter plane
8. Calvin Coolidge, Andrew Johnson, Lyndon Johnson, Theodore Roosevelt, John F. Kennedy
9. ham, chicken, beef, pork, lamb
10. *Moby Dick, Little Women, Alice in Wonderland, The Scarlet Letter, The Adventures of Tom Sawyer*
11. milk, coffee, cranberry juice, tea, cider
12. Mississippi, Fox, Rhine, Ohio, Hudson
13. bobsledding, tennis, surfing, golf, baseball
14. New York, Ohio, N. Carolina, Massachusetts, Pennsylvania
15. "God Bless America," "Beautiful Dreamer," "Yankee Doodle Dandy," "Stars and Stripes Forever," "Greensleeves"
16. nickel, penny, quarter, peso, dime
17. pizza, chop suey, spaghetti, lasagna, ravioli
18. lion, kangaroo, giraffe, koala, elephant
19. Mexico, Germany, France, Italy, Switzerland
20. Robert Frost, Andrew Wyeth, John Steinbeck, Ernest Hemmingway, Edgar A. Poe

Answers to CLASSIFYING:

General Category	Item To Remove	Specific Sub-category
1. trees	spruce	deciduous trees
2. wars	Boer War	wars U.S. fought
3. fabrics	rayon	natural fiber fabrics/non-synthetics
4. states of U.S.	Hawaii	continental states
5. nuts	peanut	tree-grown nuts
6. automobiles	Volvo	American-made automobiles
7. aircraft	glider	motorized aircraft
8. U.S. presidents	Andrew Johnson	Presidents after 1900
" "	John F. Kennedy	Vice-Presidents, then presidents
9. meats	chicken	from four-legged animals
10. books	*Little Women*	by male authors
"	*Alice in Won . . .*	by American authors
11. beverages	milk	originated from plants
12. rivers	Rhine	U.S. rivers
13. sports	bobsledding	warm-weather sports
	surfing	land sports
14. states of U.S.	Ohio	of original thirteen
15. songs	"Greensleeves"	by American composers
16. coins	peso	U.S. coins
17. foods	chop suey	Italian foods
18. animals	lion	vegetarians
19. foreign countries	Mexico	European nations
20. creative artists	Andrew Wyeth	authors

Variation: This is rather a one-of-a-kind exercise without any real possibilities for variation. However, if students have enjoyed this particular thinking challenge, they might wish to construct classifying items of their own to test the class. These can be collected and duplicated for another worksheet. A better way, however, might be to put one on the chalkboard each day as a challenge to stump the class and teacher. This could last until students have run out of ideas. The teacher could save the best ones to expand the original sheet for another year.

Do You See What I See?

Objective: to sharpen visual perception

Materials: 8″ x 10″ black line illustrations made into transparencies
9″ x 12″ tag board and numerous small items (for the variation)

Procedure: The hardest part of this activity is finding good black and white illustrations. Unfortunately, photographs will not work, as these illustrations are to be made into transparencies for the overhead. Good line drawings are needed with quite a bit of detail in them. If you, a friend, or a student can draw, the problem is solved. If not, there are some good sources where illustrations of this size and complexity can be found. The best place is the children's section of a library. Some large books with detailed illustrations are sure to be available. They can be reproduced on the copy machine, then made into a transparency. In addition, many of the catalogs for educators (especially book catalogs) that come to the school carry some suitable illustrations. If not quite large enough, careful setting of the overhead will make the transparency fill the screen. One other source is the newspaper. A travel ad might feature a drawing of a porch, beach, sailboats, etc. An article on changing neighborhoods might feature a drawing of homes being converted to businesses, etc.

For each illustration write 12 to 15 good, true/false statements. Each one should deal with a specific detail of the picture. If coloring pencils for the overhead transparencies are available, some portions of the illustration can be colored solid. Sample statements might be similar to the following:

1. The donkey is wearing a hat.

2. There are three children in the cart.
3. One child is holding an umbrella.
4. The cart is red.

When transparencies and single copies of the true/false statements are ready, start the lesson. Students face the blank screen and sit with pencils and scratch paper. When ready, turn on the light in the overhead and project the illustration for 60 seconds. Turn the light off, and read the statements aloud to the class. Each student numbers his scratch paper and indicates whether he thinks the statement is true or false. Statements can be repeated if needed.

Then turn the overhead on again as you read the statements aloud, so students can correct their own work. Repeat this process with the second and third transparencies. If the illustrations are of equal complexity, most students will increase their percentage of right answers by the third try. If you have found one really difficult drawing, you can use it and tell the students it is a super challenge. If they enjoy the activity, they will be eager to try a really hard test and will not be upset if they miss several. Those who do well will be thrilled.

This activity shouldn't occupy a whole class period. Use it as part of a perception unit, with the variation, or with a different perception activity like the one in the chapter "Now Hear This."

Variation: Number six pieces of tag board from one to six with a large number on each piece. The numbers can be colored on with one of the transparent markers used to highlight passages of text in a book. Thus, the numbers are clearly visible, yet they are definitely a background. On each piece of tag board, glue four different lightweight objects. The following list will indicate the types of objects to glue on.

several postage stamps	a pencil stub
paperclips	an eraser
coins	a plastic flower
a piece of gum	safety pins
a matchbook	colored Lifesaver candy
a Band-Aid	a school pass or library card

two crayons	bottle caps or pull tabs
fabric scrap	drinking straws
a plastic fork	a photograph
buttons	section of plastic ruler
portion of a map	lace paper doily
a key	Monopoly (or game) money

The items should be common and easy to recognize from a distance. Students in front seats will have a slight advantage as they will see better.

To participate, each student should have a scratch paper and pencil. The number-one card is held up for ten seconds and then put down. Students must then write down what the four objects were. You must decide how specific you want the answers to be. For example, will *money, coins, four coins,* or *a dime and three pennies* all be acceptable answers or will only the last two count? The ability of the class may determine how exact each answer should be. More able students should give better answers.

For the second round, card two is held up for eight seconds and followed immediately by card three for the same length of time. After viewing, not during, students write down the items. You then check the second series. You might want students to list just the eight items, or you might want them to indicate which items were on which card.

The third series includes the last three cards, in order, for five seconds each. Again check the answers. Students who did well might share their methods for remembering their technique. Ask which item was hardest to remember, or take a quick, informal poll. Were there any associations that made some cards easier to remember? Which item was easiest? Was any item easy to remember because it paired off with another one?

Several days later present all six cards at once in a scrambled order for five seconds each. Ask students to analyze their individual performances to see if they did better or worse. Let them discuss the advantages of having had the cards before. If desired, all six cards can be presented on several consecutive school days to see if performance improves. It's interesting to see how many students learn through repetition. To see how much is retained, run the card through again several months later.

Now Hear This!

Objective: to sharpen listening skills

Materials: short, factual articles (not current)

Procedure: Most teachers repeat themselves so often they sometimes begin to wonder if students ever listen. Maybe students need
practice. Beginning a few classes every now and then with a listening activity can help the situation.

To do this, collect a few short articles (under five minutes in
length when read aloud) that contain numerous facts. Try to find
articles from unfamiliar sources. Back issues of magazines two or
more years old are the best sources. Also, backs of record albums
sometimes contain factual accounts of the recording process or an
instrument, such as an unusual organ used in the recording. Book
jackets contain good, brief biographical sketches. Small pamphlets
that come with unusual gifts or works of art also offer possibilities.

For each selection, work out a set of true/false statements (see
chapter "Do You See What I See?" for samples). At the beginning
of a class period, ask students to take out scratch paper and pencils,
but insist that they only listen during the reading. Read the selection through once. Then read the true/false statements as students
indicate their choices on the scratch paper. Correct the papers and
read the selection again. In a few days, repeat the process with a
different selection. Be sure the selections are on different subjects
so that no student will have the advantage of having a similar
subject used again and again. Third, fourth, and even fifth selections can be used after brief intervals.

Improving listening skills is a worthwhile goal in itself, but this
kind of activity can also be incorporated in a perception unit or as a
pre-writing experience before doing some sensory writing.

Variation: This listening activity can also be used as training in note-taking. In this case encourage students to take notes during the reading. Teach them to jot down a word or two that restates the main idea or specific point. Articles that describe numbered steps or parts are especially effective. The numbers alert the note-taker to important points. Students should be allowed to use their notes during the test, but after two or three times, some may want to try the test without notes.

Experiment In Communication

Objective: to demonstrate the need for exact language to com-
municate effectively
to encourage students to use specific detail in their
speech and writing

Materials: 12 manila file folders
12 sheets of typing paper with simple designs on them
(Model Spirit Master 13)

Procedures: Begin the experiment by having the class define
communication. Ask them what elements are necessary for human
communication. Bring the discussion to the conclusion that three
things are necessary for communication:

> one person to send a message
> one person to receive the message
> the message itself

Tell students they are going to participate in an experiment that
demonstrates this conclusion. Ask for a volunteer to be a sender,
another to be a receiver, and the rest to get out scratch paper. Have
ready, but out of sight, the file folders each with a design inside.
Explain the directions carefully as the experiment will break down
if not followed exactly.

The sender is to stand at the back of the room with his back to the
class at all times. He will have one of the folders that he must keep
as nearly closed as possible, just peeking in to see the design
himself. He will give directions to the receiver whose task it is to

reproduce the design as he interprets the directions. The sender is not allowed to see how the design is progressing.

The receiver stands at the chalkboard at the front of the room and does whatever he thinks he has been told to do. His speech is restricted to one utterance—O.K. After he has received an instruction and carried it out, he says, "O.K.," to let the sender know he is ready for the next direction. He cannot get any help from the class either.

The class folds the scratch paper into fourths to use one section at a time. Class members also try to reproduce the design. They must keep total silence. Neither can they try to help the receiver at the board by gestures or by showing their papers. Knowing looks and raised eyebrows are allowed between class members and the teacher. The class members will have to resist the temptation to copy what the receiver is drawing; they should make their own interpretations.

The folders will contain simple designs like these:

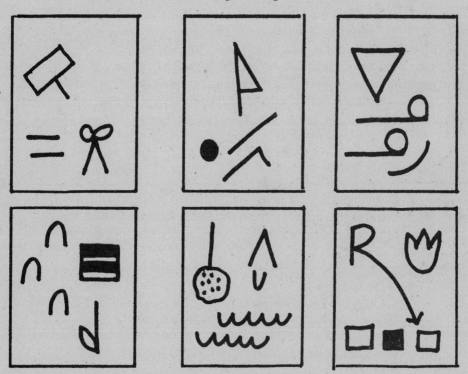

No attempt is made to rank the designs in order of difficulty, and folders are just handed out randomly to the volunteer senders. Obviously, there is no right or wrong side up to the designs either.

When the receiver has said his last O.K., the sender turns around and holds his design sheet up next to the chalkboard drawing. Comments will be swift: "You said square, and that's a rectangle. Why didn't you say color it in? You should have said...etc." Students begin to see the need for exact words. The sender and receiver each select the next pair, and the experiment is repeated. The second sender will try to be much more precise, but usually a new problem arises. If the sender directs the receiver to make a vertical line, and the receiver doesn't know what *vertical* means, a new problem appears. The receiver cannot ask for an explanation. The sender goes right on assuming he has been understood. Sizes and special relationships reveal another problem in understanding. Each new experiment offers some chance for comment and learning.

The teacher will probably tire of this long before the class will. To keep the teacher involved, a student can make a new design (unknown to the teacher) to be transmitted. The teacher takes a turn at the board as receiver, acts as a sender, or just draws along with the class. One danger in doing this is that students tend to make the designs too complicated. Be sure not to use up the entire class period as a little more discussion is needed.

To conclude the lesson, the class should try to analyze why their communications broke down in some cases. They had the three elements noted earlier — a sender, a receiver, and a message. Students should see that care is needed in choosing exact language. Also both sender and receiver must have a common meaning for the terms. It is fruitless to instruct someone to draw an equilateral triangle, if that term has no meaning to the drawer. It is useless to say to make something *big* without some point of reference. If all these problems arise between speakers of the same language and the same generation, students will see how difficult communication can become between peoples of dissimilar backgrounds.

The experiments should increase students' awareness of problems in communicating. Many will be conscious of them in their